IRIS
Folding

Stylish Greeting
Cards

Maruscha Gaasenbeek

FORTE PUBLISHERS

Contents

ISBN 90 5877 630 1

This is a publication from
Forte Publishers BV
P.O. Box 1394
3500 BJ Utrecht
The Netherlands

For more information about the creative books available from Forte Uitgevers:
www.forteuitgevers.nl

Final editing: Gina Kors-Lambers, Steenwijk, the Netherlands
Photography and digital image editing: Fotografie Gerhard Witteveen, Apeldoorn, the Netherlands
Cover and inner design: BADE creatieve communicatie, Baarn, the Netherlands
Translation: Michael Ford, TextCase, Hilversum, the Netherlands

Preface

It is with great pleasure that I present to you *Iris Folding, stylish greeting cards*.

The paper which is used to fill the new patterns in this book comes from a number of different countries and can be purchased in paper specialty stores, often via the Internet. Why don't you spend a day shopping for paper with one of your friends in the city?

Iris folding offers boundless possibilities: fill the patterns with modern colours and you will always end up with a contemporary card. Copy the asymmetric shapes the other way round, for a change, using a light box and surprise yourself and others with some different cards. Use any colourful and foldable paper that you can find, but, more importantly, have fun selecting the colours and enjoy the folding and sticking.

This is the tenth book about the technique of Iris folding. Collect them all! Thank you for your loyal and overwhelming enthusiasm for the technique of Iris folding that has no boundaries.

Kind regards,

Maruscha

Techniques

The starting point for Iris folding is the pattern. Cut the outline of the pattern out of the back of your card and then fill the hole from the outside to the inside with folded strips of paper. You work at the back of the card, so you work, in fact, on a mirror image. When you have finished the Iris folding, stick the card onto another card. For a square shape, select, for example, four different sheets of paper whose patterns and colours combine and contrast each other nicely. Cut all the paper into strips in the same way, for example, from left to right. Depending on the pattern, you will need between four and eight strips. The width of the strips also depends on the pattern and is stated for each card. You need to first fold the edge of the strips over and then sort them into the different colours. Next, cover each section in turn by following the numbers (1, 2, 3, 4, 5, etc.) using a different colour each time. Lay the strips down with the fold facing towards the middle of the pattern and stick the left and right-hand sides to the card using adhesive tape. Finally, use an attractive piece of holographic paper to cover the hole in the middle.

The basic pattern - The diamond

(See the bottom right-hand corner of page 8 and card 1 on page 9.)

It is important to start with the basic pattern, because from this, you will learn the unique folding and sticking technique needed for all the patterns. You will notice that you quickly get used to the technique of Iris folding.

Preparation

1. Lay the violet card (13.5 x 8 cm) down with the back facing towards you.
2. With the aid of a light box, copy the diamond onto the card using a pencil and cut it out.
3. Stick a copy of the diamond shown in this book (pattern 1) to your cutting mat using adhesive tape.
4. Place the card with the hole on the pattern (you should be looking at the back of the card) and *only* stick the left-hand side of the card to your cutting mat using masking tape.
5. Select four different sheets of paper. One red envelope, one blue envelope, origami paper with blue lilies and paper with red castles have been used for the card in the bottom right-hand corner of page five.
6. Cut *2 cm wide* strips from these pieces of paper and make separate piles of colour A, colour B, colour C and colour D.
7. Fold the edge of each strip over (approximately 0.7 cm wide) *with the nice side facing outwards.*

Iris folding

8. Take a folded strip of colour A and place it upside down over section 1, exactly against the line of the pattern with the folded edge *facing towards the middle.* Allow 0.5 cm to stick out on the left and right-hand sides and cut the rest off. By doing so, the strip will also slightly stick out over the edge of the pattern at the bottom, so that section 1 is totally covered.

9. Stick the strip to the card on the left and right-hand sides using a small piece of adhesive tape, but remain 0.5 cm from the edge of the card.
10. Take a strip of colour B and place it on section 2 of the pattern. Tape the left and right-hand sides to the card.
11. Take a strip of colour C. Place this on section 3 and stick it into place.
12. Take a strip of colour D. Place this on section 4 and stick it into place.

13. Start again with colour A on section 5, colour B on section 6, colour C on section 7 and colour D on section 8.

The strips on sections 1, 5, 9 and 13 of this pattern are all of colour A. The strips on sections 2, 6, 10 and 14 are all of colour B. The strips on sections 3, 7, 11 and 15 are all of colour C. The strips on sections 4, 8, 12 and 16 are all of colour D.

Finishing

Carefully remove the card after finishing section 16. Stick a piece of holographic paper in the middle on the back of the card. You can use punches, figure scissors and bits of paper to add extra finishing touches to the card. Stick small pieces of double-sided adhesive tape along the edges or use foam tape to bridge the height difference. Remove the protective layer from the double-sided adhesive tape and stick your design on a double card. Do not use glue, because all the paper strips place pressure on the card.

Punch cards

When using punch cards, the order in which you make the card may differ to that given in the book. For cards where you cut out the pattern yourself, the separate, cut-out parts are stuck on at the end, whilst the parts are covered first for punch cards. For that you need a big piece of paper that you do not fold and that you cut to size only on the same side as the strip.

Step-by-step

1. A boundless choice of beautiful paper which can be used for Iris folding.

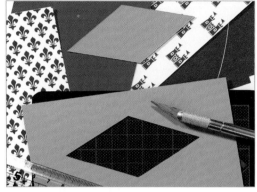

2. Cut the diamond out of the back of a piece of card.

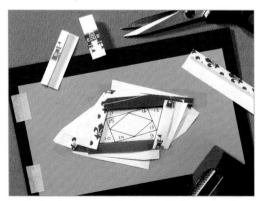

3. Cut the chosen paper into strips and fold a border along the entire length of each strip. Stick the pattern to your cutting mat. Place the card on top and tape the left-hand side to the cutting mat.

4. Place the fold of the strips exactly against the line and stick down the left and right-hand sides using adhesive tape. Fold the card open from time to time to see whether the patterns continue nicely.

Materials

To make the cards:
- Card: Canson Mi-Teintes (C), cArt-us (cA), Papicolor (P) and Romak (R)
- Knife and cutting mat
- Ruler with a metal cutting edge (Securit)
- Adhesive tape
- Double-sided adhesive tape
- Foam tape
- Masking tape
- Various corner punches (MakeMe!, Fiskars, Reuser, Carl and Lim)
- Border ornament punches (Fiskars)
- Scissors and silhouette scissors
- Corner scissors (Fiskars)
- Hole punch
- Black fine-liner
- Photo glue
- Light box

Iris folding
Strips of:
- Used envelopes
- Iris folding paper (IF paper)

English and Italian paper from Damen (D) and Vlieger (V) (50 x 70 cm or 70 x 100 cm)
- Japanese paper
- Origami paper from Ori-Expres (O-E)
- Gift paper

The middle of the card
- Holographic paper

The patterns:
Full-size examples of all the patterns are given in this book. Use a light box to copy the outline on the card. The shapes are usually easy to cut out. Special punched cards are available for the duck, the sweet jar, the dragonfly, the cross pattern and the Christmas decoration.

Diamonds

Card 1 - Basic pattern

Card: white 14.8 x 21 cm and violet 13.5 x 8 cm (P20)
• Pattern 1 • 2 cm wide strips: red envelope, dark blue envelope, blue lily origami paper (12103 from O-E) and red castles (13 vrs 007 from D) • Silver holographic paper

Cut the diamond out of the smallest card.
After completing the Iris folding, cut a red strip and a blue strip (13.5 x 2 cm). Use photo glue to stick the strips on the card so that 0.4 cm protrudes over the edge and stick it on the double card.

Card 2

Card: Christmas red 14.8 x 21 cm (P43), night blue 13.5 x 9 cm (P41) and white 13 x 8 cm • Pattern 1
• 2 cm wide strips: 2x dark blue Japanese paper and 2x gold IF paper (green set) • Gold holographic paper
Fill alternate sections with gold and dark blue paper.

Card 3

Card: night blue 14.8 x 21 cm (P41), white 13.4 x 8.5 cm and fiesta red 12.8 x 8 cm (P12) • Pattern 1
• 2 cm wide strips: 2x blue/white Japanese paper
and 2x blue envelope • Silver holographic paper
• Multi-corner punch

Card 4

Card: white 14.8 x 21 cm and dark blue 13.5 x 9 cm (cA417) • Pattern 1 • 2 cm wide strips: 2x blue IF paper, light blue envelope and blue flower pattern (ts 14 from D) • Silver holographic paper • Multi-corner punch
Punch two corners of the blue card and cut the diamonds out of the back 1 cm from the side and 1.2 cm from the top and bottom.

Card 5

Card: old red 14.8 x 21 cm (cA517), gold 13 x 8.5 cm (P102) and white 13 x 8.5 cm • Pattern 2 • 2 cm wide strips: 2x green IF paper, 2x orange IF paper and 4x

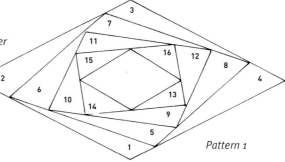

Pattern 1

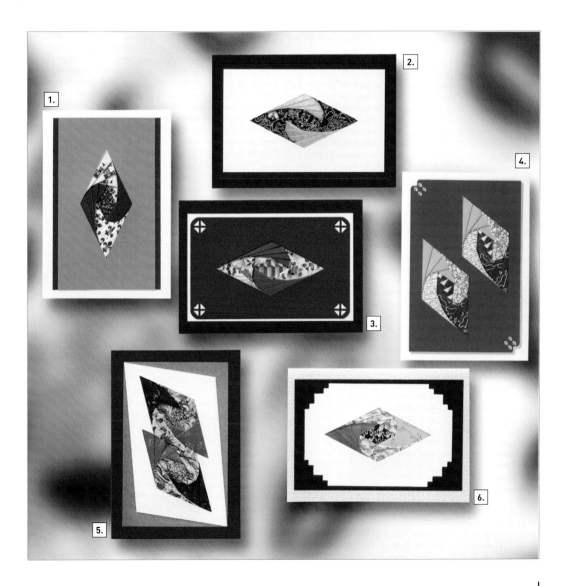

Florentijn paper in various colours (22 crt 012 from D)
• *Gold holographic paper*
Cut the diamonds out of the white card 1.2 cm from all the sides. Put a dot 1.5 cm from the top right-hand corner and bottom left-hand corner and cut all the sides of the card at an angle from these points. Fold a strip of Florentijn paper (6 x 1.4 cm) so that it measures 6 x 0.6 cm and use it to cover both no. 1 sections. Continue the Iris folding as explained for the basic model.

Card 6

Card: goldline 14.8 x 21 cm (P301), dark red 13.5 x 8.8 cm (cA519) and white 12 x 8 cm • Pattern 1 • 2 cm wide strips: aqua IF paper, 2x aqua Florentijn paper (12063 from O-E) and gold origami paper (13031 from O-E) • Gold holographic paper • Art Deco corner scissors

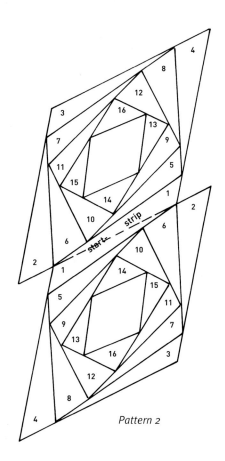

Pattern 2

Duck and bib

The duck is made according to the instructions given for card 1 and the bib is made according to the instructions given for card 3.

for the head (section 2) double. Cut the water, use the hole punch to punch the eye and stick them on the card.

Card 1

Card: warm pink 14.8 x 21 cm (cA485), white 13.5 x 9 cm and light blue 11 x 8.3 cm (cA391) • Pattern 3 • 2 cm wide strips: pink origami paper (13008 from O-E), petrol IF paper (aqua set) and 2x aqua Florentijn paper (12063 from O-E) • 5 x 4 cm piece of pink paper for the head • Gold holographic paper • Multi-corner punch • Hole punch

Punch the bottom corners of the white and blue card and cut the duck out of the blue card. Fold the paper

Card 2

Card: violet 14.8 x 21 cm (cA425), soft yellow 13 x 9.3 cm and lavender 12.6 x 9 cm (cA487) • Pattern 3 • 2 cm wide strips: yellow envelope, purple origami paper (12031 from O-E), green duck and green waffle (13 vrs 015 and cp 187 from D) • 5 x 4 cm piece of yellow paper for the head • Gold holographic paper • Multi-corner punch • Hole punch

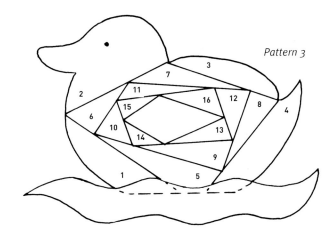

Pattern 3

Card 3

Card: white 14.8 x 21 cm, light blue 13.4 x 9.4 cm (cA391) and pink 13 x 9 cm (cA481) • Pattern 4 • 2 cm wide strips: 3x paper with flowers (7 pai 4545 from D) and 3x light blue envelope • Silver holographic paper • Multi-corner punch • Hole punch

Punch two corners of the pink card and cut out the bib. Use flower strips to fill all the A sections from the top downwards. Use light blue strips to fill all the B sections from the top downwards. Use light blue strips and flower strips alternately to fill the other sections. Use foam tape to stick the pink card on the light blue card. Stick the press stud in the top left-hand corner of the bib.

Card 4

Card: ice blue 14.8 x 21 cm (P42), dark pink 14 x 9.7 cm (C352) and white 13.5 x 9.4 cm • Pattern 4 • 2 cm wide strips: 2x blue grey IF paper (aqua set), pink envelope, red envelope and 2x flower paper • Gold holographic paper • 3-in-1 corner punch - Heart

The strips for sections A and 1, 5, 9, etc. are flowered. The strips for sections B and 2, 6, 10, etc. are blue grey.

Card 5

Card: white 14.8 x 21 cm, light blue 12.8 x 9 cm (C490) and mint 12 x 9 (8.3) cm (cA331) • Pattern 3 • 2 cm wide strips: 4x aqua IF paper • 5 x 4 cm piece of aqua paper for the head • Silver holographic paper • Border ornament punch - Rope • Hole punch

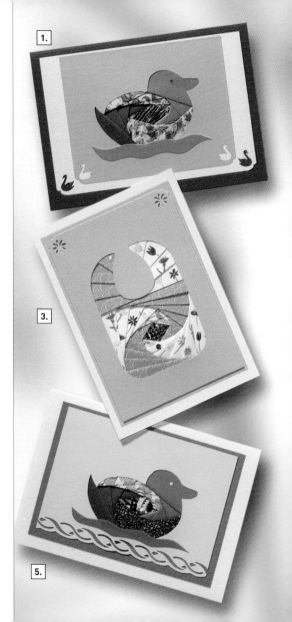

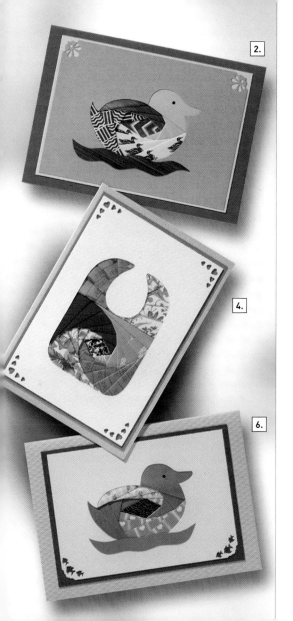

2.

4.

6.

Card 6

Card: peach 14.8 x 21 cm, warm pink 12.7 x 9 cm (cA485) and light pink 12 x 8.4 cm (C103) • Pattern 3
• 2 cm wide strips: 3x pink origami paper (13008, 13039 and 13045 from O-E) and beige envelope
• 5 x 4 cm pink origami paper for the head • Bronze holographic paper • Multi-corner punch • Hole punch

Pattern 4

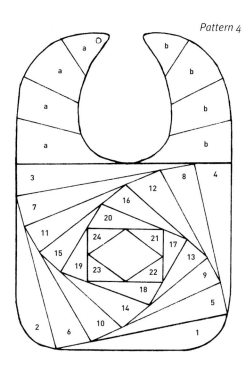

Trees and flowers

The tree is made according to the instructions given for card 1 and the cornflower is made according to the instructions given for card 3.

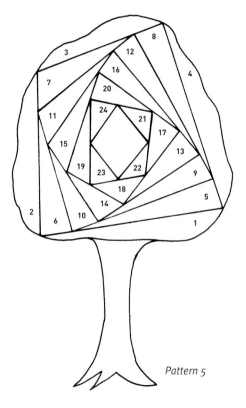

Pattern 5

Card 1

Card: cerise 14.8 x 21 cm (P33), Christmas green 14 x 9.5 cm (P18) and white 13.4 x 9 cm • Pattern 5 • 2 cm wide strips: green IF paper, green leaf origami paper (12103 from O-E), green envelope and green/beige Tassotti paper (1715 from V) • 5 x 3 cm piece of green paper for the trunk and 3 x 2 cm piece of red paper for the apples • Green holographic paper • Figure punch - Apple • Corner punch - Apple

Punch the corners of the white card. Cut out the crown of the tree and fill it with strips. Cut the trunk, punch the apples and stick them on the card.

Card 2

Card: violet 14.8 x 21 cm (P20), lime green 13 x 9 cm (P188) and white 12.5 x 8.5 cm • Pattern 5 • 2 cm wide strips: 2x green IF paper, lilac IF paper (purple set) and purple lavender branches (7 tas 1731 from D) • Purple holographic paper • Corner punch - Spear

Card 3

Card: fresh green 13 x 26 cm (P130), fern green 11.5 x 11.5 cm (P137) and white 11 x 11 cm • Pattern 6 • 3 cm wide strips: 4x yellow origami paper (12012, 12023, 13008 and 13037 from O-E) • Gold holographic paper • 3-in-1 corner punch - Flowers

Punch the corners of the white card and cut out the flower. Stick small pieces of double-sided adhesive tape to the back of the card near the four small crosses. Fill the cornflower with strips.

Card 4

Card: mustard yellow 13 x 26 cm (P48), water blue 11 x 11 cm (P131) and soft yellow 10.5 x 10.5 cm (P132)
• Pattern 6 • 3 cm wide strips: 4x blue IF paper • Silver holographic paper • 3-in-1 corner punch - Leaves

Card 5

Card: cerise 13 x 26 cm (P33), bright pink 11 x 11 cm, Christmas red 10.6 x 10.6 cm (P43) and blossom 10.2 x 10.2 cm (P34) • Pattern 6 • 3 cm wide strips: 4x pink carnation origami paper (12012, 12027, 1254 and 13039, from O-E) • Red holographic paper

Card 6

Card: mustard yellow 14.8 x 21 cm (P48), dark blue 13 x 9 cm (P06) and white 12.5 x 8.5 cm • Pattern 5 • 2 cm wide strips: yellow IF paper, green origami paper (13045 from O-E) and 2x tulip paper (cp 931 from D) • Gold holographic paper • 3-in-1 corner punch - Flowers

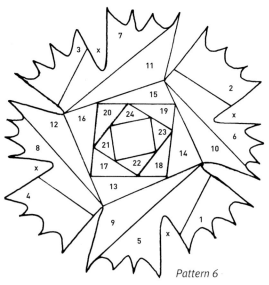

Pattern 6

Sweet jar

All the cards are made according to the instructions given for card 1.

Card 1

Card: water blue 14.8 x 21 cm (P131), old red 12.3 x 9.6 cm (cA517) and soft yellow 11.7 x 9.2 cm (P132)
• Pattern 7 • 2 cm wide strips: 2x blue IF paper, forget-me-not blue and plaited red (cp 712 and cp 174 from D) and red envelope • Silver holographic paper • 3-in-1 corner punch - Flowers
Punch the top corners of the yellow card. Cut out the jar without the lid or the base and fill the jar with strips. Cut the lid and the base out of blue IF paper and stick them on the card. Decorate the card with a flower. Use foam tape to stick the yellow card on the red card.

Card 2

Card: cherry red 14.8 x 21 cm (P133), white 13 x 9.7 cm and orange 12.5 x 9.2 cm (P135) • Pattern 7 • 2 cm wide strips: 2x green envelopes, yellow checked IF paper (yellow set), cherry paper and apple paper (both fruit paper from V) • Bronze holographic paper • Butterfly corner punch

Card 3

Card: spring green 14.8 x 21 cm (cA305), rust 12.8 x 9.6 cm (C504) and soft yellow 11.7 x 9.2 cm (P132)
• Pattern 7 • 2 cm wide strips: green envelope, yellow envelope, brown IF paper (yellow set) and 2x mini cakes (10 pai 4487 from D) • Gold holographic paper • 3-in-1 corner punch - Lace

Card 4

Card: yellow 14.8 x 21 cm (cA275), dark red 13.2 x 9.7 cm (cA519) and white 12.7 x 9.4 cm • Pattern 7 • 2 cm wide strips: paper with sweets (pink carnation, aqua, orange, green and yellow) (10 tas 204 from D) and pink carnation envelope paper • Gold holographic paper • Corner scissors - Nostalgia
Use the corner scissors to cut two corners of the white card and cut out the jar. After completing the Iris folding, stick half a sweet on the card.

Card 5

Card: apple green 14.8 x 21 cm (C475), lime green 12.5 x 9.4 cm (P188) and white 11.2 x 9 cm • Pattern 7 • 2 cm wide strips: 3x green IF paper, blue IF paper and blue envelope • Green holographic paper • 3-in-1 corner punch - Lace

Card 6

Card: cream 14.8 x 21 cm (cA241), golden yellow 12.4 x 9.4 cm (cA247) and violet 12 x 9 cm (P20) • Pattern 7 • 2 cm wide strips: 2x yellow IF paper, purple IF paper, beige envelope and purple envelope • Gold holographic paper • Circle template
Draw five circles (Ø 1.7 cm) for the lollies and cut 1.5 mm wide cream pieces of card for the sticks.

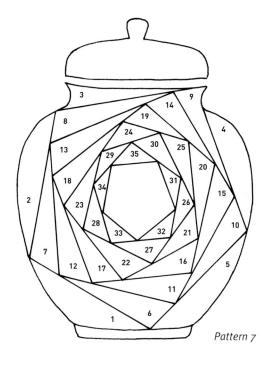

Pattern 7

1.

2.

3.

4.

5.

6.

Dragonfly

Card 1 (card on the cover)

Card: mustard yellow 13 x 26 cm (P48), dark green 12 x 12 cm (cA309) and white 11.5 x 11.5 cm • Pattern 8 • 1.5 cm wide strips: dark green IF paper (petrol set), yellow envelope and Florentijn paper in various colours (22 crt 001 from D) • 8 x 3 cm piece of green paper for the body • Gold holographic paper • 3-in-1 corner punch - Bugs

Punch the top right-hand corner of the white card. Only cut the wings out of the back of the white card and fill them with strips. Use a light box to copy the body and stick it on the front of the card.

Card 2

Card: cornflower blue 13 x 26 cm (cA393), mauve 12 x 11.5 cm (P13), warm pink 12 x 10.5 cm (cA485) and white 11.5 x 10 cm • Pattern 8 • 1.5 cm wide strips: red envelope, aqua IF paper and aqua Colourful de luxe IF paper • 8 x 3 cm piece of red envelope for the body • Silver holographic paper • 3-in-1 corner punch - Flowers

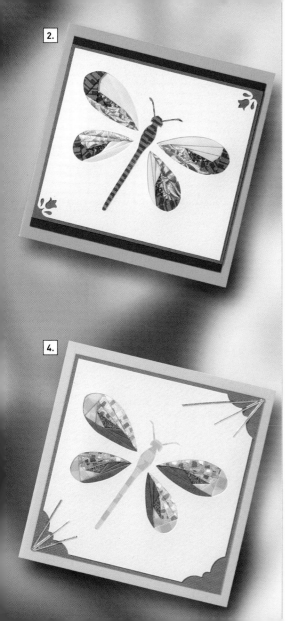

Card 3

Card: royal blue 13 x 26 cm (P136), azure 12 x 12 cm (P04) and white 11.5 x 11.5 cm • Pattern 8 • 1.5 cm wide strips: 2x blue envelope and sea green envelope • 8 x 3 cm piece of blue paper for the body • Sea green holographic paper • Border ornament punch – Rope

Cut the top right-hand and bottom left-hand corner of the white card at an angle 0.5 cm from the corner and punch a border in the top right-hand corner and the bottom left-hand corner.

Card 4

Card: golden yellow 13 x 26 cm (cA247), grey green 11.8 x 11.8 cm and white 11.3 x 11.3 cm • Pattern 8 • 1.5 cm wide strips: 2x petrol IF paper and gold IF paper (yellow set) • 8 x 3 cm piece of petrol paper for the body • Green holographic paper • Gold decorative line stickers no. 4 • Corner scissors - Celestial

Cut three corners of the white card and cut out the wings. Decorate the card with the line stickers.

Tip: If you wish to know what the effect of the different colours will be before you start, make a copy of the pattern and use coloured pencils to colour it in. You will then quickly see what it will look like.

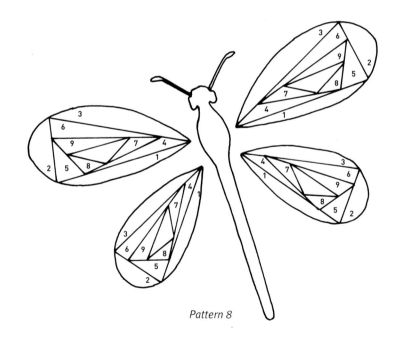

Pattern 8

Cross pattern

Card 1

Card: ochre 14.8 x 21 cm (cA575) and cream 10.2 x 9.4 cm (cA241) • Parchment: dark yellow 14.8 x 10 cm (1644) • Pattern 9 • 1.5 cm wide strips: dark brown IF paper (orange set), light brown IF paper (yellow set) and old pink/beige Tassotti (1714 from V) • 10 x 2 cm piece of dark brown paper • Gold holographic paper • Border ornament punch - Lace

Cut the four sections out of the smallest card and fill them with strips. Draw one triangle on the piece of brown paper (10 x 2 cm) and fold the strip double twice. Use a staple to keep it in place and cut the four triangles in one go. Stick them on the front of the card. Use the border ornament punch to decorate the top and bottom of the parchment.

Card 2

Card: dark blue 13 x 26 cm (cA417), light blue 11 x 11 cm (C490) and shell white 10.5 x 10.5 cm (C112) • Pattern 9 • 1.5 cm wide strips: blue envelope, grey green origami paper (13039 from O-E) and blue vine (cp 81 from D) • 10 x 2 cm piece of blue paper for the triangles • Silver holographic paper • 3-in-1 corner punch - Lace

Card 3

Card: pale pink 13 x 26 cm and 10.5 x 10.5 cm (cA480), salmon 11.5 x 11.5 cm (cA482) and terracotta 11 x 11 cm (cA549) • Pattern 9 • 1.5 cm wide strips: brown origami paper (11008 from O-E), grey envelope and brown grey cord pattern (mg 010 from D) • 10 x 2 cm piece of brown paper for the triangles • Gold holographic paper • 3-in-1 corner punch - Leaves

Card 4

Card: wine red 14.8 x 21 cm (P36), twilight grey 14 (13) x 9.2 cm (C131) and pale pink 10.5 x 9.2 cm (cA480) • Pattern 9 • 1.5 cm wide strips: 3x purple IF paper • 10 x 2 cm piece of purple paper for the triangles • Silver holographic paper • Border ornament punch – Leaf

Cut the four sections out of the smallest card and use the border ornament punch to decorate the top and bottom of the grey card.

Card 5

Card: dark green 14.8 x 21 cm (cA309) and cream 12.5 x 9.5 cm (cA241) • Pattern 9 • 1.5 cm wide strips: green IF paper, denim green origami paper (1254 from O-E) and green/beige Tassotti (1715 from V) • 10 x 2 cm piece of green paper for the triangles • Gold holographic paper • 3-in-1 corner punch - Leaves

Pattern 9

Christmas decorations and candles

The Christmas decorations are made according to the instructions given for the card on the cover and the candle is made according to the instructions given for card 4.

Card on the cover

Card: ochre 14.8 x 21 cm (cA575), dark green 13 x 9 cm (cA309) and white 12.5 x 8.5 cm • Pattern 10 • 2 cm wide strips: yellow IF paper, green IF paper and green/beige Tassotti (1715 from V) • Gold holographic paper • Corner scissors - Nostalgia

Decorate the corners of the white card with part of the scissors and cut the Christmas decoration out. Cut the eye out of green paper and stick it on the card. Use foam tape to stick the white card on the green card.

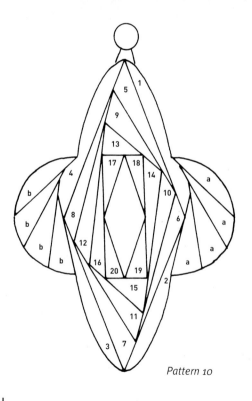

Pattern 10

Card 1

Card: iris blue 14.8 x 21 cm (P31) and white 13 x 9 cm • Silver holographic paper - Honeycomb (EmJe) 13.3 x 9.3 cm • Pattern 10 • 2 cm wide strips: 2x sea green gift paper, 2x purple gift paper and 2x honeycomb silver holographic paper • Silver holographic paper • 3-in-1 corner punch - Snowflakes

Card 2

Card: dark green 14.8 x 21 cm (cA309), cerise 13 x 9 cm (P33) and white 12.5 x 8.5 cm • Pattern 10 • 2 cm wide strips: green IF paper (petrol set), green beige Tassotti (1715 from V) and yellow envelope

• *Pink square holographic paper* • *10 cm of pink thread* • *Corner scissors - Nostalgia*

flower pattern (ts 14 from D) • *6 x 3 cm piece of lilac paper for the flames* • *Silver holographic paper*

Card 3

Card: violet 14.8 x 21 cm (P20) and white 12.2 x 8.7 cm • Dark red envelope 12.8 x 9.2 cm • Pattern 10 • 2 cm wide strips: 2x purple gift paper, 2x dark red envelope and 2x holly silver holographic paper (EmJe) • Purple holographic paper • 3-in-1 corner punch - Lace

Card 4

Card: red, triple square aperture card 14.8 x 21 cm (192-23 from R) and red 14.5 x 10.2 cm • Pattern 11 • 1 cm wide strips: 2x beige leaf origami paper (14040), gold and red/beige stripes (both 13031 from O-E) • 6 x 3 cm piece of gold paper and 4.5 x 2 cm piece of leaf paper for the flames • Gold holographic paper • Gold decorative line stickers no. 4
Fill each square with strips and cover the back with the single card. Copy the big flame onto the strip of gold paper. Fold it into three and cut out the flames in one go. Make the small flames in the same way. Stick the line stickers and the flames on the card.

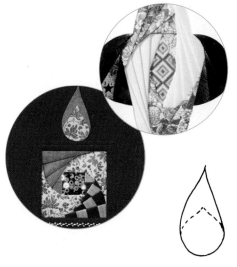

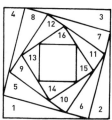

Card 5

Card: blue, triple square aperture card 14.8 x 21 cm (192-25 from R) and blue 14.5 x 10.2 cm • Pattern 11 • 1 cm wide strips: 2x lilac gift paper and 2x blue

Pattern 11

Small star and robin redbreast

Card 1

Card: blue 13 x 26 cm, mustard yellow 10.5 x 10.5 cm (P48), pale yellow 10 x 10 cm and dark blue 8 x 8 cm (C500) • Pattern 12 • 2 cm wide strips: yellow envelope, pale yellow envelope and gold paper (V)
Cut out the star from the smallest card.

Card 2

Card: dark blue 13 x 26 cm (P06), white 10 x 10 cm, turquoise 7.3 x 7.3 cm (P32) and mustard yellow 7 x 7 cm (P48) • 10 x 10 cm pale yellow parchment (1645) • 2 cm wide strips: white envelope, blue envelope and sea green gift paper • Silver holographic paper • Border punch - Star
Punch all the borders of the parchment and stick it on the white card.

Card 3

Card: cream 13 x 26 cm (cA241), dark blue 11 x 11 cm (cA417) and violet 7.2 x 7.2 cm (P20) • Pattern 12 • 2 cm wide strips: yellow envelope, beige envelope and yellow IF paper • Gold holographic paper • Gold decorative line stickers no. 4 • 3-in-1 corner punch - Celestial

Card 4

Card: dark red 14.8 x 21 cm (cA519), ochre 12.2 x 8.4 cm (cA575) and white 11 x 8 cm • Pattern 13 • 2 cm wide strips: orange envelope, grey white envelope and brown grey cable pattern (mg 010 from D) • Black paper for the eye and beak • Gold holographic paper • Hole punch • Black fine-liner • Corner punch - Holly
Punch two corners of the white card and cut out the bird without the beak. Use a light box to copy the feet onto the back of the card. Turn the card over and use a fine-liner to draw them on the front of the card. Sections 1A, 1B, 4A, 4B, 4C, 7A, 7B and 10 are brown grey, sections 2, 5, 8, 11A and 11B are orange and sections 3, 6A, 6B, 9A, 9B, 12A, 12B and 12C are grey white. Use the hole punch to punch the eye, cut out

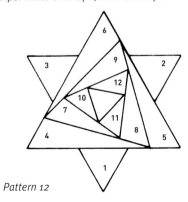

Pattern 12

a beak and stick them on the card. Use foam tape to stick the white card on the ochre card.

Card on page 1

Card: dark blue 14.8 x 21 cm (C500), rust 11.5 x 9.2 cm, mustard yellow 10.7 x 8.3 cm (P48) and white 10.8 (9.6) x 8.3 cm • Pattern 13 • 2 cm wide strips: grey white envelope, orange origami paper (12031 from O-E) and brown IF paper (orange set) • Mother-of-pearl holographic paper • Border ornament punch - Holly

Card 5

Card: ochre 14.8 x 21 cm, dark blue 11.3 x 9.4 cm (P06), orange 10.7 x 8.9 cm (cA545) and white 10.2 x 8.5 cm • Pattern 13 • 2 cm wide strips: grey white envelope, brown origami paper (12054 from O-E) and orange origami paper (12031 from O-E) • Bronze holographic paper • Corner punch - Carl

Card 6

Card: dark chestnut 14.8 x 21 cm (C501), raw sienna 12 x 9 cm (C374), red earth 10 x 9 cm (C130) and white 10 (8.8) x 9 cm • Pattern 13 • 2 cm wide strips: brown IF paper (orange set), grey envelope and orange envelope • Silver holographic paper • Border ornament punch - Holly

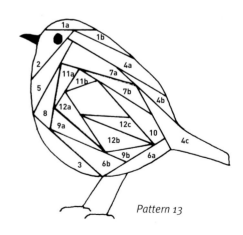

Pattern 13

Many thanks to
- Kars & Co BV in Ochten, the Netherlands.
- Damen, Papier Royaal in The Hague,
  the Netherlands
- Pergamano International in Uithoorn,
  the Netherlands
- Ori-Expres in Reusel, the Netherlands

The materials used can be ordered by
shopkeepers from:
- Kars & Co BV in Ochten, the Netherlands
  (www.kars.biz)
- Papicolor International in Utrecht,
  the Netherlands.
- Em-Je B.V. in Zuidwolde, the Netherlands
- Pergamano International in Uithoorn,
  the Netherlands

Card-makers can purchase the paper from:
- Damen, Papier Royaal at Noordeinde 186 in
  The Hague, the Netherlands
  (www.papier-royaal.nl)
- Ori-Expres in Reusel, the Netherlands
  (www.ori-expres.nl)
- Vlieger at Amstel 34 in Amsterdam,
  the Netherlands